FROM SEA to SHINING SEA

CONNECTICUT

NANCY FURSTINGER

Consultants

MELISSA N. MATUSEVICH, PH.D.
Curriculum and Instruction Specialist
Blacksburg, Virginia

BINA WILLIAMS, M.L.S.
Bridgeport Public Library
Bridgeport, Connecticut

CHILDREN'S PRESS®
A DIVISION OF SCHOLASTIC INC.

New York · Toronto · London · Auckland · Sydney · Mexico City
New Delhi · Hong Kong · Danbury, Connecticut

Connecticut is in the northeastern United States. It is bordered by Rhode Island, Massachusetts, New York, and Long Island Sound.

The photograph on the front cover shows a tall ship at Mystic Seaport.

Project Editor: Meredith DeSousa
Art Director: Marie O'Neill
Photo Researcher: Marybeth Kavanagh
Design: Robin West, Ox and Company, Inc.
Page 6 map and recipe art: Susan Hunt Yule
All other maps: XNR Productions, Inc.

Library of Congress Cataloging-in-Publication Data

Furstinger, Nancy.
    Connecticut / Nancy Furstinger.
        p. cm. – (From sea to shining sea)
        Contents: Introducing the Constitution State—The land of Connecticut—Connecticut
through history—Governing Connecticut—The people and places of Connecticut—
Connecticut almanac—Timeline—Gallery of famous Nutmeggers—Glossary.
    ISBN 0-516-22324-0
    1. Connecticut—Juvenile literature. [1. Connecticut.] I. Title. II. Series.

F94.3 .F87 2002
974.6—dc21   2001006980

TABLE of CONTENTS

CHAPTER ONE

INTRODUCING THE CONSTITUTION STATE

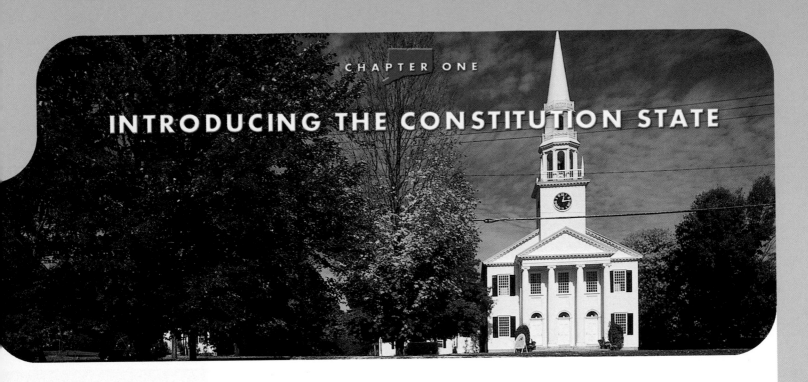

In autumn, the town green in Litchfield is a picture-perfect New England scene.

Connecticut nestles in the northeastern corner of the United States. It welcomes visitors to the New England region, which also includes Maine, Massachusetts, New Hampshire, Rhode Island, and Vermont. New England has a scenic beauty all its own. You may have seen photos of colorful autumn trees, or a small town blanketed in snow; these photos were probably taken in New England.

Slicing through Connecticut's scenic landscape, the Connecticut River divides the state in half. Native Americans called the river *Quin-nehtukqut,* meaning "beside the long tidal river." If you say the river's name quickly, you'll hear how English settlers named their new home.

Connecticut is also sometimes called the Constitution State. The United States' first written constitution was adopted in Connecticut in 1639. This set of laws determines the duties of the government and the rights of the people.

Another nickname for Connecticut is the Nutmeg State. Nutmeg is a spice used to flavor baked goods, including pumpkin pies. According to legend, crafty peddlers (the first door-to-door salespeople) in colonial Connecticut sold useless nutmegs whittled from wood. Others believe that buyers wrongly cracked the nutmegs in half (nutmeg should be grated, not cracked), and then falsely accused peddlers of selling useless "wooden" nutmegs.

However the names were derived, these events are only part of Connecticut's history. It stretches as far back as 200 million years ago, when a three-toed dinosaur called Eubrontes lived in Connecticut. Today, visitors can make plaster casts of the dinosaur's footprints that were left behind.

What else comes to mind when you think of Connecticut?

- Floating down the Connecticut River on an inner tube
- Exploring a nineteenth-century whaling town at Mystic Seaport
- Playing Frisbee® on the lawn at Yale University
- Watching the Bluefish play baseball in Bridgeport
- Going down the hatch at the Naval Submarine Base

Connecticut has many interesting surprises. In this book, you'll read about some of the people and events that have shaped the Constitution State.

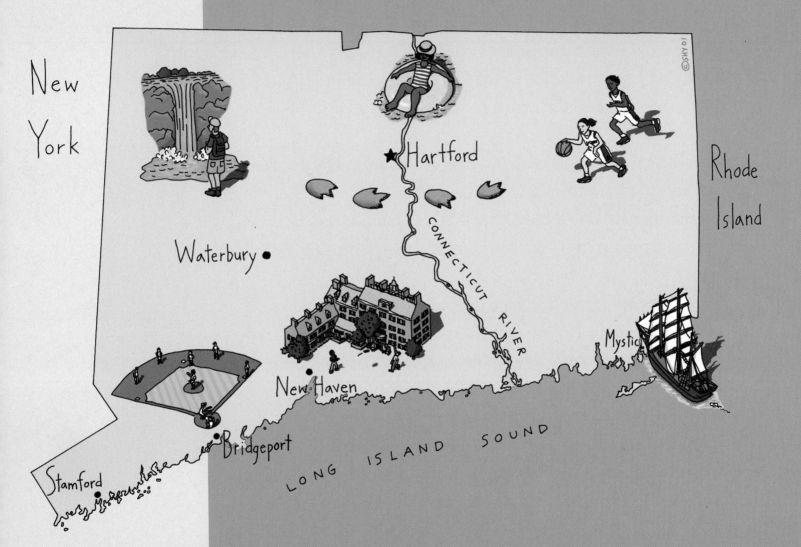

Massachusetts

New York

Rhode Island

★ Hartford

Waterbury ●

CONNECTICUT RIVER

New Haven

Mystic

Bridgeport

Stamford

LONG ISLAND SOUND

CHAPTER TWO

THE LAND OF CONNECTICUT

Connecticut is the third smallest state, yet it is more than four times the size of its tiny next-door neighbor, Rhode Island. You could zip around Connecticut's borders in one day. Along the coast, you'll find sandy beaches. Out in the harbor you may sight a sperm whale—the creature with the biggest brain on record. If you go inland, you can explore thick forests and rolling hills, or cast dinosaur tracks in the valley. Remember to bring your raincoat. A Nor'easter storm may strike!

Connecticut is 101 miles (163 kilometers) from east to west, but only 73 miles (117 km) from north to south. Its outline forms a rectangle with a handle in the lower-left corner. Connecticut contains a total area of 5,544 square miles (14,359 square kilometers). It is bordered by Rhode Island to the east, Massachusetts to the north, and New York to the west. A narrow channel of water called Long Island Sound runs along the southern border of Connecticut.

Connecticut's scenic beauty includes an abundance of trees and meandering rivers.

7

COASTAL LOWLANDS

New Haven's Lighthouse Point Park is a public swimming beach on the coast of Long Island Sound.

The Coastal Lowlands run along Connecticut's southern coast on the Long Island Sound. Rocky ridges and pebbly beaches rise from the water's edge. Short, flat peninsulas jut out into shallow bays. Boats anchor in harbors at Bridgeport, New Haven, New London, Mystic, and Stonington, home of the state's only remaining fishing fleet.

(CONNECTICUT VALLEY LOWLANDS)

The Connecticut River shaped the fertile valley, called the Connecticut Valley Lowlands, in the middle of the state. Over time, river water carved out the lowlands and deposited rich topsoil in the valley. The lowlands begin in the harbor at New Haven and extend north into Massachusetts. Rocky ledges rise above the river valley, forming Mount Carmel, Avon Mountain, and Ragged Mountain.

If you've visited New York City, perhaps you saw a chunk of Connecticut's lowlands. Many city row houses, called brownstones, were built of reddish brown sandstone, a mixture of quartz and iron, from the lowlands. Today, sandstones are commonly used in paving stones and grindstones.

Farms such as this one are nestled in the fertile valley of the Connecticut River.

9

EASTERN NEW ENGLAND UPLAND

The Eastern New England Upland is located in the northeastern portion of the state. Hills and valleys run in a north-south direction to form the Eastern Upland, where the elevation rises up to 1,200 feet (366 meters). The rounded hills of Norwich resemble petals of a rose, giving the city its nickname: The Rose of New England. Branches of the Thames River drain the upland, while the lower Connecticut River spans the southwestern portion.

WESTERN NEW ENGLAND UPLAND

Hilly forests, sweeping valleys, and marble rock formations shape the Western Upland, located in the western part of Connecticut. The low mountains of the Litchfield Hills merge with the Berkshires in Massachusetts, separated by the Housatonic River, which flows southward through Connecticut. A portion of the Appalachian Trail, a footpath running from Maine to Georgia, follows a stretch of the river before continuing into Massachusetts.

The town of Salisbury, near the northwestern portion of the trail, was once famous for its iron ore used to fashion anchors, cannons, and chains during the American Revolution. Farther south, in Roxbury, people mined both granite and garnets—jewels that look like red-hot coals. Granite quarries there provided stone for New York's Grand Central Terminal.

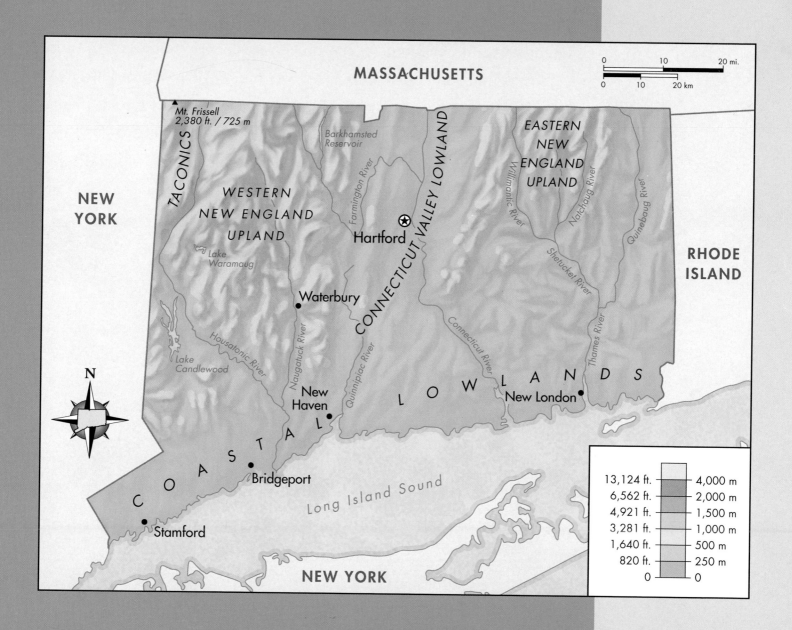

MASSACHUSETTS

Mt. Frissell
2,380 ft. / 725 m

TACONICS

WESTERN
NEW ENGLAND
UPLAND

Barkhamsted
Reservoir

EASTERN
NEW
ENGLAND
UPLAND

NEW
YORK

Lake
Waramaug

Farmington River

Hartford

CONNECTICUT VALLEY LOWLAND

Willimantic River

Natchaug River

Quinebaug River

RHODE
ISLAND

Housatonic River

Lake
Candlewood

Waterbury

Naugatuck River

Quinnipiac River

Connecticut River

Shetucket River

New London

L O W L A N D S

Thames River

New
Haven

C O A S T A L L O W L A N D S

Bridgeport

Long Island Sound

Stamford

NEW YORK

| 0 | 10 | 20 mi. |
| 0 | 10 | 20 km |

13,124 ft.	4,000 m
6,562 ft.	2,000 m
4,921 ft.	1,500 m
3,281 ft.	1,000 m
1,640 ft.	500 m
820 ft.	250 m
0	0

N

If you want to climb to the highest point in Connecticut, head for the Taconic Mountain range in the northwest corner. Climb 2,380 feet (725 m) up Mount Frissel or scale 2,355-foot (718-m) Bear Mountain in Salisbury, the highest mountain peak entirely within Connecticut's borders. State parks dot the region, including Kent Falls State Park, where hikers can climb a woodland path beside the 250-foot (76-m) waterfall.

Kent Falls State Park draws thousands of visitors each year.

RIVERS AND LAKES

Water forms a big part of Connecticut. Long Island Sound laps on the southern coast. The Sound is an estuary, where salt water from the Atlantic Ocean mixes with fresh water from inland sources. It is a long body of water that stretches 253 miles (407 km) along the Connecticut coast.

About 8,400 miles (13,519 km) of rivers and streams crisscross the state. The longest river, the Connecticut, starts in Third Connecticut Lake in New Hampshire. It flows southward for about 407 miles (655 km), dividing Connecticut in half and passing by Hartford, the capital city. About one-fifth of the river lies within Connecticut's borders. The river empties into Long Island Sound.

Other large rivers in Connecticut include the Farmington, Housatonic, Naugatuck, Thames, and Quinnipiac Rivers. Settlers used the swift-flowing rivers to turn waterwheels, thereby creating water-power to manufacture goods such as cotton cloth and ship cannons. Settlers also transported cargo along rivers, a practice that continues today. Salmon and shad splashed in streams, supplying settlers with fish to eat and sell. However, when cities sprung up along the rivers, water

The Connecticut River flows through four states—New Hampshire, Massachusetts, Vermont, and Connecticut.

pollution became a huge problem. Cleanup efforts have helped the salmon to make a comeback.

Thousands of lakes and ponds dot the state. Humans created Connecticut's largest lake, Candlewood Lake. This reservoir covers about 8 square miles (21 sq km) and supplies both water and power. Located above Danbury, Candlewood is the third largest man-made lake in the eastern United States. You can swim, fish, canoe, and ice-skate there.

Lake McDonough, located in Barkhamsted, provides recreational opportunities all year round.

CLIMATE

While Connecticut has a moderate climate, temperatures change with the four seasons. Summers are usually warm, around 80° Fahrenheit (27° Celsius). Winter temperatures average about 31°F (−1C°). The average temperature may vary about 6 degrees from north to south. The greatest temperature contrast occurs in the winter.

Connecticut's weather may surprise you. Someone once described New England weather by saying, "If you don't like it, just wait a minute. It will change." A sudden change could mean a Northeaster (popularly called a Nor'easter). Nor'easters are windstorms that bring heavy rain or snow as well as strong winds. Each year about 20 inches (51 centimeters) of rain and 25 inches (64 cm) of snow fall in Connecticut.

Hurricanes sometimes blow in from the ocean and continue inland. In September 1938, the New England Hurricane struck. Scientists tracked the storm across Long Island in New York and then up the Connecticut River to Vermont and New Hampshire. Winds in excess of 100 miles per hour (161 kilometers per hour) lashed the central and southern New England coastline, and

FIND OUT MORE

People once believed the village of Moodus, located in south central Connecticut, was haunted. They heard shrieks and noisy blasts coming from the ground. Settlers blamed the scary sounds on witches, while Native Americans credited spirits. Today, scientists know that fault lines join together under Moodus. When these underground rocks suddenly slip past each other, earthquakes occur. Why does the ground groan as it settles?

EXTRA! EXTRA!

The Blizzard of 1888 dropped 31 inches (79 cm) of snow on New Haven in just one day. By the time the storm was over, 45 inches (114 cm) covered the city. The snowstorm, which took people by surprise, caused trains to stop running and businesses to shut down for several days. More than 400 people across the East Coast died in the blizzard.

The waterfront area of New London was devastated after the New England Hurricane of 1938.

heavy rains flooded the Connecticut River Valley. In its wake, the hurricane left millions of dollars in damages and 85 Connecticut residents dead. It was one of the most powerful and destructive storms ever to strike New England.

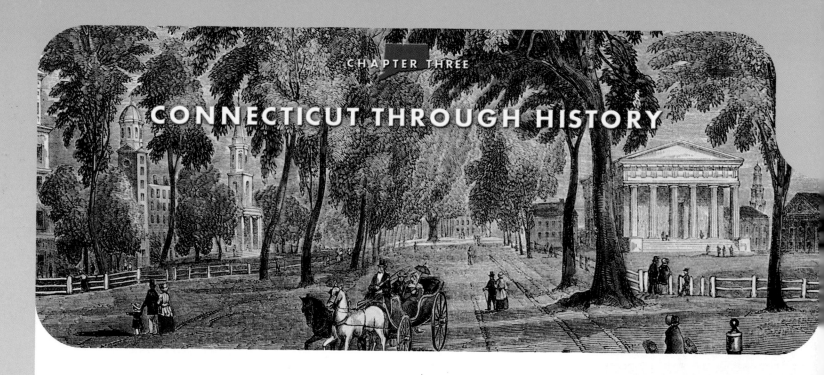

CHAPTER THREE

CONNECTICUT THROUGH HISTORY

About 200 million years ago, dinosaurs ruled the land we now call Connecticut. The last dinosaurs died out 64 million years ago, long before humans existed. However, they left their tracks behind. More dinosaur tracks have been found in the Connecticut Valley than any other place in the world.

The Ice Age began two million years ago. This was a time when large areas of Earth were covered with sheets of sea ice or glaciers. As the glaciers retreated, the melting waters spread out to form lakes, and swept boulders into mountains. In New England, Earth's crust sank 300 to 800 feet (91 to 244 m) from the heavy weight of the ice sheet, forming valleys.

Yale College (shown above) made New Haven one of New England's most prosperous cities during the late 1700s and early 1800s.

EXTRA! EXTRA!

In 1966, 2,000 dinosaur tracks were discovered in a layer of sandstone in Rocky Hill, Connecticut. After measuring the size and shape of these footprints, scientists determined that the tracks belonged to a meat-eating, three-toed dinosaur called Eubrontes. Many of the tracks can be seen at Dinosaur State Park, where they are enclosed under a dome for viewing.

Eventually the ice melted, and the land thawed and became green. Enormous animals such as mastodon began wandering north. Giant saber-toothed tigers with knife-like teeth and packs of dire wolves stalked their prey. Today these animals are extinct, perhaps due to changes in climate or overhunting by early man.

NATIVE AMERICANS

The first humans arrived in what is now Connecticut when the Ice Age ended, about 10,000 years ago. It is likely that these early humans, called Paleo-Indians, crossed the Bering Strait, a land bridge between Asia and North America. Then they walked down from what is now Alaska. As they spread to the New England region, Paleo-Indians hunted Ice Age creatures with spears.

Over time, descendants of the Paleo-Indians settled in present-day Connecticut. These Native Americans formed various tribes, or groups, including the Mohegan, Nipmuc, Pequot, and Schaghticoke. The Mohegan and Pequot lived in the Thames River valley between Norwich and Uncasville, until the groups split in the 1630s. Then the Pequot, who were the most numerous, extended their territory from the Connecticut River to the Pawcatuck River, and as far north as the Massachusetts border. The Nipmuc occupied the northeastern corner of Connecticut, while the Schaghticoke made their home in western Connecticut.

These Native Americans, members of the Eastern Woodland tribes, built houses called wigwams from hickory trees covered with bark. Stones were made into tools and arrowheads. Native Americans hunted deer, fowl, and bears in the woodlands, and made dugout canoes from hollowed-out tree trunks to catch fish. They grew corn, pumpkin, squash, and beans. They also cut the bark of sugar maples and collected the sap, then boiled it to make sugar. To preserve food for the winter, they dried it on smoking racks.

Fur traders hunted and trapped beavers in many parts of the North and Northeast.

DUTCH EXPLORER, ENGLISH SETTLERS

The first European to land on Connecticut shores was Adriaen Block, a Dutch explorer from the Netherlands who arrived in 1614. Block and his crew sailed their ship, the *Onrust* (meaning "restless") up the Connecticut River, which he called *Varshe*, or "fresh." Block stepped ashore at present-day Hartford. He hoped to trade with the Pequots, exchanging trinkets such as beads for beaver furs. When Block encountered the Enfield Rapids on his voyage up the Connecticut River, he turned around and journeyed back down the river. He created a map of Connecticut, marking Xs along the coast, perhaps at good trading spots.

Word spread about the abundance of beaver furs in Connecticut. Furs were valuable in Europe, where they were fashioned into hats for the wealthy. By 1623, a group of Dutch traders from the colony of New Netherland bought land from the Pequots and built a trading post called House of Hope, near what would later become Hartford. The Dutch traded guns and other items for beaver furs.

In 1633, settlers built a fort in present-day Windsor. The following year settlers built a community in Wethersfield, the oldest permanent settlement in Connecticut. Soon, English settlers from the

nearby colony of Massachusetts also came to explore the Connecticut wilderness. Word spread about farmland in the lush valley surrounding the river. Some settlers wished to escape the crowded Boston area. Others felt that the Massachusetts government was too strict. A group of about 100 Puritans, led by Reverend Thomas Hooker, traveled south along the Connecticut River and created a colony near the Dutch trading post in what is now the city of Hartford.

Some Native Americans, such as the Quinnipiac, helped the settlers to grow food. Not everyone welcomed the newcomers, however. The Pequots did not want to give up their land. To protect their territory near the lower Connecticut River, which led to the rich beaver regions

Colonists attacked and burned a Pequot fort near present-day New Haven.

in the interior, the Pequot attacked the Narragansett, Native-American rivals who were also interested in trading with the Dutch.

A trader for the Dutch West India Company became outraged by the Pequot's attempts to control the fur trade. The trader seized a Pequot sachem, or chief, named Tatobem, and held him for ransom. When the ransom was paid with *wampum* (shell beads that Native Americans used to trade) rather than the expected beaver skins, the trader killed Tatobem. The Pequot were furious, and they attacked and burned the trading post.

The Pequot War broke out in 1637. Armed settlers lead by Captain John Mason attacked and burned a Pequot village. Clergyman Cotton Mather described the destruction of the Pequot: "The greatness and the violence of the fire. . . the shrieks and yells of men and women and children. . . It was a fearful sight to see them frying in the fire and the streams of blood quenching the same." While settlers claimed victory, the Pequots were almost destroyed.

After 1637, Europeans took over still more land in Connecticut. Many Native Americans were crowded out of their land and forced to leave the region. They received goods as payment, but often the trade was not fair. For example, in 1638, a Puritan minister bought a large chunk of land in exchange for 23 coats, 12 spoons, 24 knives, 12 hatchets, and scissors and hoes.

In time, farm villages dotted the state. Corn and wheat grew quickly in the rich soil of the valley. However, rocky, hilly fields made farming difficult. Some settlers found other ways to earn a living. Some took to the sea, building ships and hunting whales. Seafaring towns such as New London developed along Connecticut's shoreline. Others caught fish and salted it to sell. Several people mined copper for tools and kettles. The first copper in America was mined at present-day East Granby around 1709. Many residents built mills and used water to power them, making

WHAT'S IN A NAME?

Many names of places in Connecticut have interesting origins.

Name	Comes From or Means
Three Judges Cave	Named after Judges Goffe, Whalley, and Dixwell, three local judges who hid in caves to avoid being killed by King Charles II
Middlebury	Central position of the town's meeting house, 6 miles (10 km) from Waterbury, Southbury, and Woodbury
Thomaston	Named after Seth Thomas, who opened a clock shop that became the world's largest clock factory
Wolcott	Named after Lieutenant Oliver Wolcott
Ledyard	Named after Colonel William Ledyard, under whom townspeople fought during the American Revolution
Woodstock	A town in Oxfordshire, England
Suffrage	Named after the hardships settlers overcame in 1740 (now Canton)
Willimantic	Pequot word meaning "by the banks of the fast-running river"
Housatonic River	Native American word meaning "place beyond the mountains"
Lake Waramaug	Named after Chief Waramaug, a powerful warrior

Immigrants from Ireland, Italy, Poland, and other European countries made their way to Connecticut.

goods such as cloth and tools. Settlers transported their goods on the Connecticut River.

Most of the first settlers emigrated, or moved, from England. Later, many early settlers moved west, searching for better land. People from other ethnic groups replaced them. First came the Irish, fleeing from the potato famine of the 1840s. Italians, Germans, Canadians, Polish, and others followed, searching for new opportunities in Connecticut's expanding industries. Irish immigrants settled in Hartford and New Haven, the Polish in New Britain, and the Italians in Bridgeport, Middletown, New Haven, and Waterbury.

CONNECTICUT'S CONSTITUTION

Connecticut claims the first written constitution, a document that outlines government rules and regulations. This set of laws, called the Fundamental Orders, gave voters the right to elect leaders. Puritans wrote the constitution in 1639. It is considered the first document in history to establish a government by approval of the people. In 1662, the king of England gave the colonists a charter, or grant for land. The charter showed that the king approved Connecticut's government, and it allowed the colonists more control over their government.

Twenty-five years later, however, the charter was in danger. The new king, James II, united all the New England colonies under one government. He named Sir Edmund Andros as governor. Andros demanded that Connecticut give up its charter. In October 1687, leaders gathered at Sanford's Tavern in Hartford to decide what to do. Suddenly the candle-lit room went dark. When the lights came on, the charter had mysteriously vanished. Captain Joseph Wadsworth is credited with hiding it in the hollow of a large white oak tree. The tree became known as the Charter Oak.

The white oak toppled during a storm in 1856. Pieces of the Charter Oak frame the 1662 charter, which is on display at the Museum of Connecticut History in Hartford. A memorial plaque commemorates where the Charter Oak once stood. Today the tree is featured on 750 million quarters minted in 1999.

The Charter Oak became a symbol of freedom in Connecticut.

EXTRA! EXTRA!

Did you know that Connecticut once had two capitals? From 1701 to 1875, leaders met in both Hartford and New Haven. In 1875, Hartford was made the sole capital.

Colonists were furious when they read the Stamp Act.

THE COLONIES AT WAR

Throughout the 1700s, France and England struggled for control of North America. The French and Indian War (1754–1763) ended the struggle, with the British (English) victorious. Although none of the war occurred on Connecticut soil, Connecticut sent troops to help British soldiers fight against the French and the Native Americans.

During the war, the thirteen colonies became increasingly independent. Colonists formed their own troops and sold supplies to British troops. As a result, they became frustrated when, in an effort to raise money after the war, England forced the colonies to pay unfair taxes, such as the Stamp Act of 1765. The tax stamp appeared on all American-made paper goods such as newspapers and playing cards, requiring colonists to pay between a halfpenny to 10 pounds sterling to England. Colonists argued against "taxation without representation," saying it was unjust that they should pay taxes to the English government when the colonies were not represented there.

The Revolutionary War (also called the American Revolution, 1775–1783) for independence began on April 19, 1775, when British sol-

EXTRA! EXTRA!

A strange battle took place in Windham in the summer of 1758. When people heard strange sounds one night, they thought their town was under attack by an army of French and Indian troops. Townspeople armed themselves with guns, swords, and pitchforks. At dawn, confused scouts found thousands of dead frogs at a dried-up pond. The frogs had fought their own noisy battle for a tiny remaining puddle.

diers fired on Minutemen in nearby Lexington, Massachusetts. (Minutemen were a group of militia so named because they could be ready for battle in a minute.) On June 17, 1775, the Battle of Bunker Hill in Massachusetts marked the first major conflict of the war. Connecticut's governor, Jonathan Trumbull, was the only royal governor to support the colonies' fight for independence. He sent troops to fight in the revolution, along with food, guns, and ships.

When General George Washington called for a volunteer to spy

WHO'S WHO IN CONNECTICUT?

Israel Putnam (1718–1790) was brigadier general of the Connecticut militia during the Battle of Bunker Hill. He commanded his militiamen by saying, "Don't fire until you see the whites of their eyes!" Following orders, the troops waited until the English came within yards before firing. Putnam's bravery and courage served as inspiration to his troops at the battle of Bunker Hill.

on the British, Nathan Hale answered. This Connecticut hero, posing as a Dutch schoolmaster on a trip to New York, crossed enemy lines, traveling from Norwalk to Long Island to gather secret data. On his return trip, the British captured Hale and discovered the notes and maps he was carrying. They hung him without a trial. He uttered his famous last words from the gallows: "I only regret that I have but one life to lose for my country." These words came to symbolize the American spirit.

In 1780, General George Washington gave Connecticut a new nickname: the Provision State. The general and his Continental Army of

Nathan Hale was hanged by the British on September 22, 1776.

FIND OUT MORE

During the Revolutionary War, General George Washington had an accident at Bull's Bridge in Kent, when one of his horses fell into the Housatonic River. In his expense account for March 3, 1781, Washington wrote: "getting a horse out of Bull's Bridge Falls, $215.00." It must have been a time-consuming rescue mission, as $215 was a huge sum at that time. What other things might Washington have included in his expense account?

about 11,000 men were starving at Valley Forge, Pennsylvania during the winter of 1777–1778. Congress was unable to help the freezing, hungry troops, but Governor Trumbull came to their rescue. He shipped out thousands of barrels of pork, beef, salt, and flour.

Connecticut also supplied iron. Iron forges (furnaces where metal was heated and formed into shape) were used to make guns for the warship *Constitution*. At a forge in Lime Rock, workers made 3-foot (.9-m) links. When joined together, the giant chain stretched across the Hudson River at West Point in New York. This underwater chain prevented British ships from sailing up the river. The state's Colonial Copper Mine near East Granby was also used to help American forces. Washington claimed it as an army prison, renaming the mine New-Gate Prison. It became the first working state prison in the nation in 1776.

New London, the site of the earlier Pequot War, also saw action during the revolution. In September 1781, British troops under Benedict Arnold captured Fort Griswold and burned the city in an attempt to stop ship raids from the New London harbor. The British raided other Connecticut towns along the coastline, including Groton. Rather than defending their own coast, however, many Connecticut soldiers were required to help defend the Hudson River instead.

The Revolutionary War ended with the surrender of the British at Yorktown, Virginia, on October 19, 1781. Two years later, in 1783, England signed a formal treaty recognizing the independence of the American colonies. The United States was born.

STATEHOOD

In 1787, leaders signed the United States Constitution, a document which stated the laws and beliefs of the new nation's government. When the Constitution was drawn up in Philadelphia, leaders could not decide how each state would be represented. How many lawmakers would each send to Congress?

Three Connecticut delegates (representatives) offered a solution known as the Connecticut Compromise. In the Senate (a lawmaking body in the United States government), all states would be equally represented. Each state would choose two senators. The House of Representatives (another group of lawmakers within the government) would select leaders according to population. States with larger populations would select more lawmakers than those with smaller populations.

The compromise settled the issue. Delaware was the first state to ratify, or approve, the Constitution, followed by Pennsylvania, New Jersey, and Georgia. On January 9, 1788, Connecticut ratified the Constitution. It became the fifth state of the United States.

INDUSTRIAL REVOLUTION

In the early to mid 1800s, Connecticut's economy shifted from farming and trading to industry. New England was the first region in the United States to industrialize, which meant that handmade things were now mass-produced by machines. Connecticut factories churned out clocks, tools, and muskets.

Many new inventions made life easier and often changed people's way of life. Eli Whitney, a Yale graduate, invented the cotton gin in 1793. This machine picked seeds from cotton faster than 50 people could. As a result, cotton production increased in the South, making plantation owners wealthy. Later, he attempted to mass-produce muskets with interchangeable parts in his Hamden arms plant, although he was not entirely successful. Samuel Colt, born in Hartford, greatly increased the productivity of the first assembly line when he manufactured revolvers. Brothers Oliver and Horatio Ames harnessed the power of the Housatonic River to open Ames Iron Works in Falls Village, where they produced ship cannons and railroad cars.

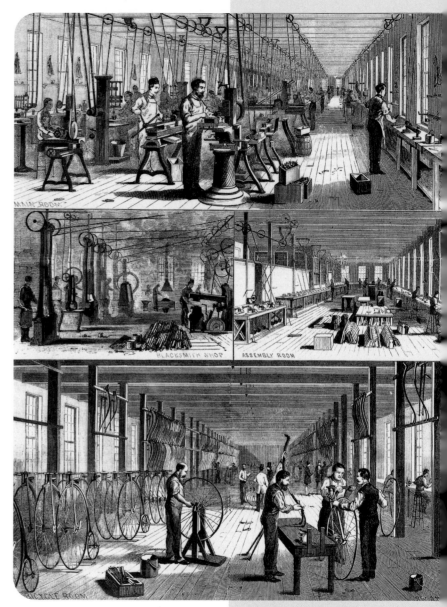

Connecticut factories turned out all kinds of goods, from sewing machines to silverware.

Charles Goodyear discovered a way to strengthen rubber.

Other inventors focused on household goods. Eli Terry made clocks in Plymouth in the 1790s. Seth Thomas's clock shop in Thomaston became the world's largest. In 1833, the cabinet and trunk lock industry began in Terryville, which became known as America's Lock Capital. A few years later, New Haven native Charles Goodyear discovered a way to strengthen rubber called vulcanization (named after Vulcan, the Roman god of fire). The process involved heating rubber with sulfur to keep it from becoming brittle in cold weather or sticky in hot weather. His discovery led to a wider use of rubber, which was later used in automobile tires.

Cotton mills sprang up in eastern towns such as Pomfret and Jewett City. Danbury became a center for hats, earning the nickname Hat City. Peddlers sold tin goods and hardware from Bristol and New Britain factories.

These products could be exported quickly and inexpensively to other regions thanks to improvements in transportation. Strong steam engines powered steamboats to Connecticut ports during the early 1800s. Steamboats carried raw goods to Bridgeport, New Haven, and New London ports. On their return trip, the boats shipped finished products.

In 1828, the Farmington Canal opened. The canal was a man-made waterway that would eventually connect New Haven with Northampton, Massachusetts. Cargoes of coffee, flour, and sugar were carried between Connecticut and Massachusetts in only 24 hours. However, the canal closed in 1847 due to costly repairs and competition from railroad lines.

In 1837, the first railroad in Connecticut started operating between Stonington and Providence, Rhode Island. In 1848, a rail line linked New Haven with New York City. More than a dozen railway companies started in the state during the mid 1800s.

This drawing by Edward Lamson Henry shows a rush of people arriving to meet the 9:45 train in Stratford.

FAMOUS FIRSTS

These Connecticut inventions and innovations made life easier, tastier, colorful, and more fun:

- The oldest U.S. newspaper still published is the *Hartford Courant*, established in 1764
- The first magazine for children, *The Children's Magazine*, was published in Hartford in 1789
- The graham cracker was created by West Suffield minister Sylvester Graham in 1829
- The country's first amusement park was built in Bristol in 1846
- The first sewing machine was built by Elias Howe in Litchfield Hills, patented in 1846
- Evaporated milk was created by Gail Borden of Torrington in 1856
- The first football game was played at Yale in 1873
- The first telephone book, containing fifty names, was published in New Haven in 1878
- The first three-ring circus was staged by P. T. Barnum at Bethel in 1881
- The first hamburger was made at Louis' Lunch in New Haven in 1895
- The helicopter was designed by Igor Sikorsky of Stratford in 1939
- Wiffle balls were invented by David Mullany of Fairfield in 1953

EXTRA! EXTRA!

The first American patent (an official document that declares ownership of an invention) issued to a woman was awarded to a Connecticut resident. In 1809, Mary Kies of South Killingly invented a machine that wove straw and silk. If you lived in the 1800s, what invention might you have created to make life easier? What might you invent now?

Around the same time, Mystic harbor, on Connecticut's southeastern coast, became a shipbuilding center. Clipper ships and whalers were handcrafted there. Whalers hunted the sperm whale almost to extinction. Whale oil was used to light lamps. Sealing ships journeyed to Patagonia, bringing back fur seal pelts.

Seaports led to a new trade in Connecticut. Shipowners worried about fires, storms, and wrecks ruining their cargoes. Pirates were also a threat to ships carrying molasses, spices, and rum from the West Indies. To protect themselves, shipowners banded together to share the risks. Owners paid money into a common fund to cover losses. In turn, they shared the profits when a ship returned safely. In this way, Hartford's insurance industry was born.

Today, Hartford is nicknamed "Insurance City" because companies such as the Hartford Insurance Company (formed as the Hartford Fire Insurance Group in 1810), Aetna Life and Casualty Company, and the Travelers Corporation are headquartered there.

Although the industrial revolution changed life mostly for the better, there was a downside. Children as young as six years old now worked in factories and operated machines for up to fourteen hours a day. Toxic fumes made workers ill and dangerous machinery and working conditions often caused injuries. In addition, wages were so low that employees earned barely enough to make a decent living.

In an effort to improve working conditions, workers began to unite. In 1833 a strike took place in Thompsonville, when carpet weavers called for higher wages. Striking employees refused to go to work. In South Norwalk, more than one thousand hatters also went on strike in 1884 when their wages were decreased. Some improvements were made as a result of these protests.

FIGHTING SLAVERY

Back in the early 1700s, when Connecticut was a colony, wealthy families owned slaves. Slaves were Africans who were kidnapped from their homeland and brought to North America on ships. There they were bought and sold as property, mainly to wealthy southern landowners. Slaves were forced to do backbreaking work on farms, and they were punished for trying to escape from their owners.

Connecticut enforced laws against slavery in 1784, which made the buying and selling of slaves illegal within the state. Slaves who were already in Connecticut were freed when they reached the age of 25.

In 1839, the Spanish slave ship *Amistad* set anchor in Long Island Sound. The ship was taking 53 Africans to market, where they would be sold into slavery. The slaves on board, including one boy and three girls, had been snatched from their families in Mendeland, on the west coast of Africa. After being chained for two months on the crowded ship, the Africans revolted. They used nails to free themselves from their iron collars and gained control of the ship. They were arrested and charged with murder and mutiny, then imprisoned in New Haven to await trial.

A scene from the movie *Amistad* shows Africans in chains on board a Spanish slave ship.

Connecticut citizens and abolitionists (people who wanted to end slavery) helped the Africans in their two-year legal battle. Eventually, the United States Supreme Court freed the surviving 37 Africans and they returned home to Africa.

Many people in Connecticut helped slaves escape to freedom on the Underground Railroad. This was a secret network of people and places to help slaves reach freedom safely. People in Hartford set up hiding stations along the railroad, aiding slaves in their journey to Canada. Connecticut finally ended slavery in 1848. In 1850, 7,693 of approximately 370,792 Connecticut residents were freed slaves.

Slaveowners often hunted down runaway slaves, who used the Underground Railroad to escape to freedom.

Although slavery was abolished (ended) in the northern states, it still continued in the South. In the North, many people worked in factories and were paid wages. Slavery was illegal in many parts of the North. In the South, however, cotton plantations operated through slave labor. Without the unpaid work of slaves, the plantation system would fall apart.

The issue of slavery helped to fuel the Civil War (1861–1865), which pitted the North (the Union) against the South (the Confederacy). More than 57,000 soldiers from Connecticut fought for the Union. Once again Connecticut was the Provision State. Factories sent out uniforms, muskets, military wagons, and ships. Between 1860 and 1870, production in Connecticut almost doubled. When the war ended in 1865, the North was victorious.

After the Civil War, nearly four million southern slaves were finally free. Some attended free schools that were set up to teach reading and writing. Others worked as sharecroppers or tenant farmers, who gave a share of crops raised to their landlord. Some moved north to states such as Connecticut, in search of better opportunities.

WORLD WARS, SHIPS, AND SUBMARINES

The state's economy boomed again during World War I (1914–1918). Although this international war started in Europe, the United States declared war on Germany on April 6, 1917. Connecticut supplied guns and bullets to help the war effort, and about 67,000 Connecticut citizens fought in the war overseas. World War I ended when Germany asked for a peace treaty on November 11, 1918.

The Great Depression struck in October 1929, when the stock market crashed. Many people all over the United States suffered financial difficulties after losing money in the stock market. In Connecticut, the industrial economy suffered. Across the nation, prices plunged, banks closed, and unemployment spread, leaving thousands without jobs. It took many years before the economy recovered.

The start of World War II (1939–1945) helped to bring the nation out of the Depression. About 210,000 Connecticut citizens fought in the war against Germany. Once again, wartime goods were in demand, and Connecticut factories responded by building submarines, airplane engines, and propellers. For the first time, many women worked in these factories, filling in for men who were fighting overseas.

Women worked in place of men in Connecticut's gun factories during World War II.

Today, two branches of the nation's armed forces are in Connecticut. The United States Coast Guard Academy moved to New London in 1910. Members of the Coast Guard train to protect United States waters. In 1917, the United States Navy's Submarine Base opened in Groton. The first Navy submarine, the USS *Holland,* was built in Connecticut by Electric Boat in 1900. In 1954, the USS *Nautilus,* the first atomic submarine, launched in Groton. However, the submarine was never used in war.

PEACETIME

Connecticut continued making wartime supplies during peacetime. For defense purposes, the state produced arms, space hardware, missiles, and airplane engines. Other factories switched to making goods such as electronics. Some companies left the state. For example, textile mills moved south, where labor was cheaper and cotton closer.

Cities and suburbs swelled during the 1950s, and the population in Connecticut grew twice as fast as all of New England. About 2,007,000 people called Connecticut home in 1950. African-Americans and Hispanics settled in Connecticut to take advantage of new job opportunities. To handle growth, the Connecticut Turnpike opened in 1958. This 129-mile (208-km) route crosses the state from Greenwich to Killingly.

In the 1960s, companies began moving from New York City to the suburbs of Connecticut, where rent was cheaper. Stylish shops opened, and the riverfront area in Hartford was restored to its original splendor. Parks offered a spot to relax while boats sailed past.

From 1950 to 1970, about one million people moved into Connecticut from elsewhere. This surge in population caused environmental problems. The many industries and cars polluted the air, and cities along rivers polluted the water. In the 1970s, state leaders focused on the environment, passing the Environmental Policy Act. This act requires an environmental review of state-funded projects, which helps to avoid those projects that might affect Connecticut's air or water in a negative way.

A worker tests for water pollution in Long Island Sound.

Further changes took place in the 1990s. The Mashantucket Pequot opened a huge gambling casino in 1992. Called Foxwoods Casino, it quickly became the most successful casino in the world. Foxwoods employs thousands of people, both tribal members and non-tribal members. Another Native American tribe, the Mohegan Tribal Nation, opened a rival casino called Mohegan Sun in 1996.

Eleven thousand people work at Foxwoods, the largest resort casino in the world.

In 1997, the Freedom Trail attracted even more people to Connecticut. When the film *Amistad* opened, tourists flocked to the trail, which links 36 sites in Connecticut that relate to African-Americans' struggle for freedom. Visitors can see buildings that were used to hide slaves on the Underground Railroad, sites connected to the Amistad trial, and gravesites and monuments associated with the concept of freedom.

Today, Connecticut is in the midst of another transformation. Just as manufacturing replaced agriculture in the mid 1800s, the manufacturing sector is being replaced by the growing biotechnology industry. Biotechnology is a field of science that studies ways to improve farming and industrial processes by working with cells. A $40 million state program provides loans to companies opening high-tech laboratories in Connecticut. According to Governor John G. Rowland, "Anything we can do to make Connecticut a bio-tech leader will have a continuing positive impact on the overall economic health of our state." Thanks to its residents who work hard and think creatively, Connecticut has a bright future ahead.

CHAPTER FOUR

GOVERNING CONNECTICUT

The capitol building houses offices for the governor, lieutenant governor, and the legislature (Connecticut's lawmaking body).

(opposite)
Legislators gather to discuss the passing of new laws.

Connecticut's government today works almost as it did more than 350 years ago. The plan for its government is laid out in the constitution, which divides the state government into three branches, or parts: the executive, the legislative, and the judicial.

EXECUTIVE BRANCH

The executive branch enforces state laws. The governor is head of the executive branch. He or she offers ideas for new laws and changes to current laws. The governor also signs bills—written drafts of new laws—such as those to create jobs and cut taxes. After natural disasters, the governor seeks federal aid—monies to assist people in need and to repair damages.

The governor is one of six people in the executive branch who is elected by Connecticut residents. Other elected officials are the lieutenant governor, secretary of state, treasurer, comptroller, and attorney general. These officials help support the governor. All six state officers serve four-year terms and may be reelected.

LEGISLATIVE BRANCH

The legislative branch creates new laws and changes old laws. For example, the legislature might pass a law that protects Connecticut's air and water from pollution, or provides funds for the building of new schools or roads. A proposed new law, called a bill, must be agreed upon by a majority of the legislature.

The legislative branch, called the General Assembly, is divided into two parts: the senate and house of representatives. In 2001, there were 36 state senators and 151 state representatives, all of whom are elected to serve two-year terms.

JUDICIAL BRANCH

The judicial branch interprets laws through the court system. Connecticut has four types of courts: the supreme court, appellate court, superior court, and probate court. Many cases begin in superior court. One hundred and fifty judges across the state listen to 750,000 cases each year. Criminal cases (those involving breaking the law), family cases (those involving family or children's issues), and civil cases (cases in which two parties are in disagreement over the meaning of a law) are some of the matters heard in superior court. If a person is found guilty of committing a crime, a judge or jury determines the punishment. Probate courts handle cases involving parenting, adoptions, and wills and estates.

If someone is not satisfied with the outcome of their case, they may request that it be heard in the appellate court or in the state supreme court, which is Connecticut's highest (most important) court. A chief justice (judge) and six judges hear cases on the supreme court. The governor selects the judges for eight-year terms. Lawyers present cases on behalf of their clients, and decisions are made a few months after a case is heard.

CONNECTICUT STATE GOVERNMENT

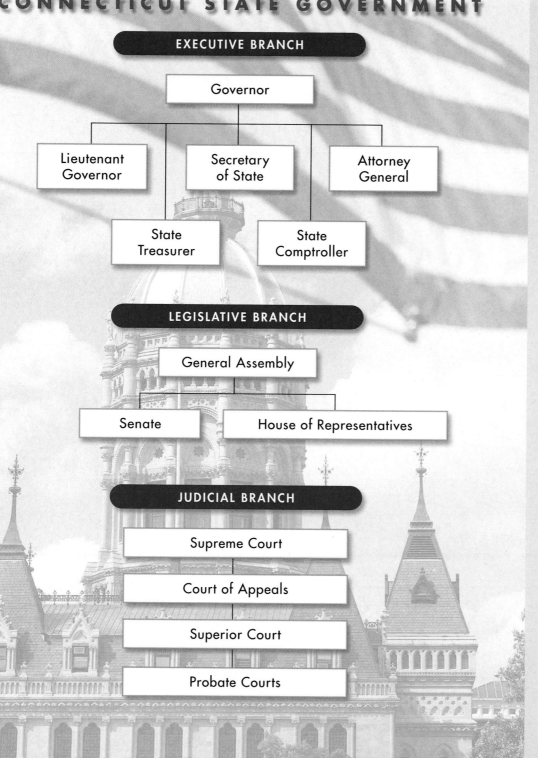

EXECUTIVE BRANCH

Governor

Lieutenant Governor

Secretary of State

Attorney General

State Treasurer

State Comptroller

LEGISLATIVE BRANCH

General Assembly

Senate

House of Representatives

JUDICIAL BRANCH

Supreme Court

Court of Appeals

Superior Court

Probate Courts

CONNECTICUT GOVERNORS

Name	Term	Name	Term
Jonathan Trumbull	1776–1784	Henry B. Harrison	1885–1887
Matthew Griswold	1784–1786	Phineas C. Lounsbury	1887–1889
Samuel Huntington	1786–1796	Morgan G. Bulkeley	1889–1893
Oliver Wolcott	1796–1797	Luzon B. Morris	1893–1895
Jonathan Trumbull Jr.	1797–1809	O. Vincent Coffin	1895–1897
John Treadwell	1809–1811	Lorrin A. Cooke	1897–1899
Roger Griswold	1811–1812	George E. Lounsbury	1899–1901
John Cotton Smith	1812–1817	George P. McLean	1901–1903
Oliver Wolcott, Jr.	1817–1827	Abiram Chamberlain	1903–1905
Gideon Tomlinson	1827–1831	Henry Roberts	1905–1907
John S. Peters	1831–1833	Rollin S. Woodruff	1907–1909
Henry W. Edwards	1833–1834	George L. Lilley	1909
Samuel A. Foot	1834–1835	Frank B. Weeks	1909–1911
Henry W. Edwards	1835–1838	Simeon E. Baldwin	1911–1915
William W. Ellsworth	1838–1842	Marcus H. Holcomb	1915–1921
Chauncey F. Cleveland	1842–1844	Everett J. Lake	1921–1923
Roger S. Baldwin	1844–1846	Charles A. Templeton	1923–1925
Isaac Toucey	1846–1847	Hiram Bingham	1925
Clark Bissell	1847–1849	John H. Trumbull	1925–1931
Joseph Trumbull	1849–1850	Wilbur L. Cross	1931–1939
Thomas H. Seymour	1850–1853	Raymond E. Baldwin	1939–1941
Charles H. Pond	1853–1854	Robert A. Hurley	1941–1943
Henry Dutton	1854–1855	Raymond E. Baldwin	1943–1946
William T. Minor	1855–1857	Wilbert Snow	1946–1947
Alexander H. Holley	1857–1858	James L. McConaughy	1947–1948
William A. Buckingham	1858–1866	James C. Shannon	1948–1949
Joseph R. Hawley	1866–1867	Chester Bowles	1949–1951
James E. English	1867–1869	John Davis Lodge	1951–1955
Marshall Jewell	1869–1870	Abraham Ribicoff	1955–1961
James E. English	1870–1871	John Dempsey	1961–1971
Marshall Jewell	1871–1873	Thomas J. Meskill	1971–1975
Charles R. Ingersoll	1873–1877	Ella T. Grasso	1975–1980
Richard D. Hubbard	1877–1879	William A. O'Neill	1980–1991
Charles B. Andrews	1879–1881	Lowell P. Weicker, Jr.	1991–1995
Hobart B. Bigelow	1881–1883	John G. Rowland	1995–
Thomas M. Waller	1883–1885		

TAKE A TOUR OF HARTFORD, THE STATE CAPITAL

Hartford is the state capital and Connecticut's second largest city, with a population of 121,578. Let's start our tour with a visit to the Old State House. Built in 1796, it is the oldest state house in the country. It now houses a museum filled with information about Connecticut history. Costumed guides portray famous people in Hartford's history, and exhibits feature curiosities such as a huge alligator and a two-headed calf! Yes, both were once alive.

The Hartford skyline sparkles at night.

Today, Connecticut lawmakers meet in the gold domed state capitol building on Capitol Hill. Completed in 1878, the capitol is decorated with a carving of the Charter Oak. The dome is surrounded by six blue marble statues known as the Six Pursuits, representing agriculture, commerce and wisdom, education, force/war, justice, and music. Across the street you can visit the State Library and State Museum, which houses pieces of the original Charter Oak.

Two famous writers were neighbors in Hartford. Mark Twain built a house on Farmington Avenue that is now open for tours. Twain described the city of Hartford by saying, "Of all the beautiful towns it has been my fortune to see, this is the chief."

Mark Twain lived and worked in this Hartford house from 1874 to 1891.

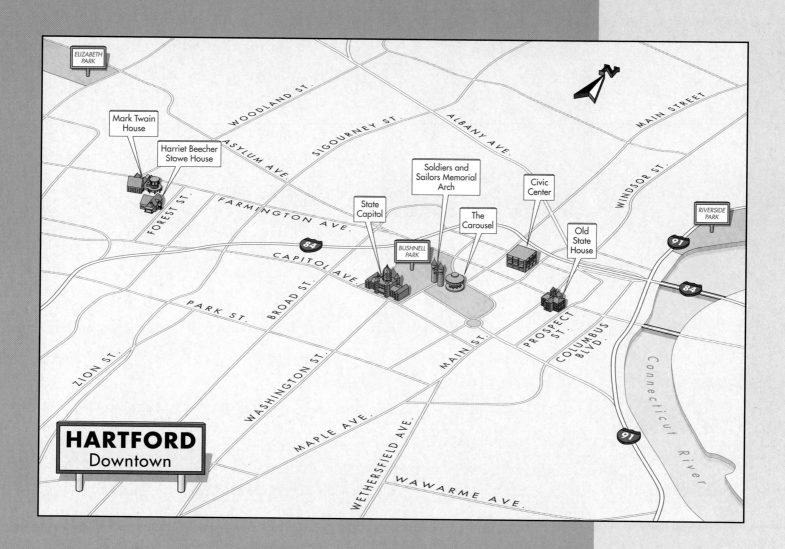

ELIZABETH PARK

Mark Twain House

Harriet Beecher Stowe House

WOODLAND ST.

SIGOURNEY ST.

ALBANY AVE.

MAIN STREET

ASYLUM AVE.

FOREST ST.

FARMINGTON AVE.

Soldiers and Sailors Memorial Arch

Civic Center

WINDSOR ST.

State Capitol

The Carousel

Old State House

RIVERSIDE PARK

84

CAPITOL AVE.

BUSHNELL PARK

91

PARK ST.

BROAD ST.

84

ZION ST.

WASHINGTON ST.

PROSPECT ST.

COLUMBUS BLVD.

91

MAIN ST.

MAPLE AVE.

WETHERSFIELD AVE.

WAWARME AVE.

Connecticut River

HARTFORD
Downtown

Next door, you can visit Harriet Beecher Stowe's cottage. Unlike Twain, Stowe wrote books in longhand while she sat on a wooden chair at a tiny table. The author moved there after writing *Uncle Tom's Cabin,* a book that turned many people against slavery. President Abraham Lincoln jokingly claimed that Stowe's antislavery book started the Civil War.

Next, spend a day looking at art in the Wadsworth Atheneum. The Wadsworth Atheneum opened in 1842 as the first public art museum. Today, its collection spans 5,000 years. Nearby, tour the Menczer Museum of Medicine and Dentistry, where you will find gadgets for pulling teeth dating back to the Revolutionary War. There's even a model of a 1919 dentist's office.

If you walk to a grassy spot in the center of bustling downtown Hartford, you'll find Bushnell Park. This 37-acre (15-hectare) park was designed by celebrated landscape architect Fredrick Law Olmsted, born in Hartford in 1822, who also designed Central Park in New York City. In the park, the Soldiers and Sailors Memorial Arch pays tribute to Hartford citizens who served in the Civil War. Nearby, a bronze, 8-foot (2.4-m) monument honors Israel Putnam, the American Revolutionary war general who commanded troops at Bunker Hill. The Corning Fountain, erected in 1899 and presented by John Corning of the Corning Glass Works of New York, recognizes his father, who operated a grist mill on that spot. Constructed of marble and stone, the fountain features a hart, or stag, surrounded by Saukiog Indians, the city's first inhabitants.

If you're tired of walking, hop aboard the Bushnell Park Carousel and listen to tunes from its Wurlitzer band organ. The carousel's 48 carved horses have been revolving since 1914. For more fun, watch the Hartford Wolf Pack hockey team take to the ice at the Civic Center.

Then, stop and smell the roses. You can sniff more than 800 varieties of roses at Elizabeth Park Rose Gardens. Take a nature walk, play lawn bowling in summer, or ice-skate in winter at Elizabeth Park. You can also enjoy terrific views of the Connecticut River as you bike along the trail of Hartford's Riverside Park.

The Soldiers and Sailors Memorial Arch is made of brownstone from Portland, Connecticut. Scenes from the Civil War are depicted across the top.

The Carousel horses are unique because of their huge, colorful roses and real horse hair tails.

CHAPTER FIVE

THE PEOPLE AND PLACES OF CONNECTICUT

Fishermen enjoy Connecticut's 253 miles (407 km) of coastline. This fishing shack is located in Niantic, near Long Island Sound.

In 2000, 3,405,565 people lived in Connecticut. If you gathered 100 Connecticut residents together, 82 would be of European descent. They are a blend of the first English settlers plus immigrants from other European countries, such as France, Ireland, Italy, and Poland. Nine of the 100 would be African-American. The rest would be Hispanic, Asian, and Native American.

Few of Connecticut's original peoples remain. The Pequot and Mohegans live on reservations, tracts of land set aside by the United States government. These Native Americans keep their culture alive through museums, crafts, and powwows, or special ceremonies. There are almost 1,000 Pequot in the state, split into two tribes: the Paucatuck, who live on the Lantern Hill Reservation at North Stonington, and the Mashantucket, who live on the Ledyard Reservation. After opening a successful gambling casino in 1992, the Mashantucket Pequot became the wealthiest Native Americans in the nation.

There are 169 towns in the state's eight counties. Most of Connecticut's population is concentrated in regions along Long Island Sound and in the Connecticut River Valley. In these regions, 80 of every 100 residents live in Bridgeport, New Haven, and Hartford—the three largest cities in terms of population. The other 20 people live in rural areas.

WORKING IN CONNECTICUT

Starting from the earliest settlements in the 1630s, nearly everyone was a farmer. Farms once covered three-fourths of Connecticut. Today, about 370,000 acres (149,734 ha) are used for growing crops, with about 4,000 farms generating $900 million in income. Farmers grow apples, corn, potatoes, and tomatoes, but the biggest cash crop is shade-grown tobacco for cigar wrappers.

Some farmers raise livestock, including beef cattle, sheep, and hogs. Others grow flowers and shrubs in nurseries, generating

There are more farms per square mile in Connecticut than in any other New England state.

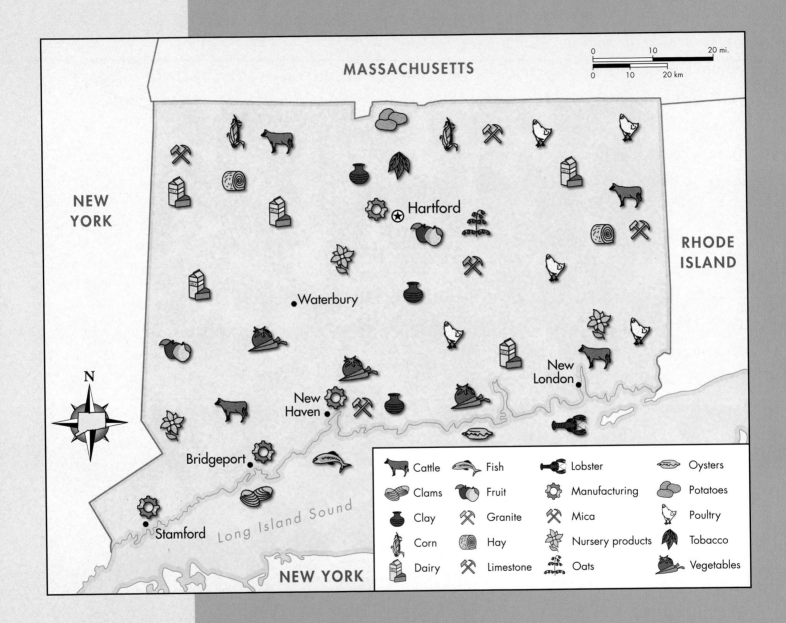

MASSACHUSETTS

NEW YORK

RHODE ISLAND

Hartford

Waterbury

New Haven

New London

Bridgeport

Stamford

Long Island Sound

NEW YORK

N

Cattle		Fish		Lobster		Oysters	
Clams		Fruit		Manufacturing		Potatoes	
Clay		Granite		Mica		Poultry	
Corn		Hay		Nursery products		Tobacco	
Dairy		Limestone		Oats		Vegetables	

0   10   20 mi.
0   10   20 km

$168 million from nursery and greenhouse production and $50 million from bedding and garden plants. Even stones are worth money. The stone walls farmers used during colonial times to border their fields now enclose yards in wealthy communities such as Greenwich and Westport.

Early settlers used their skills to make things people needed. Today, Connecticut workers continue to manufacture products. Factories supply the military with transportation equipment. Aircraft engines, helicopters, missiles, and submarines roll off assembly lines. Computers and machine tools are shipped around the globe. Workers make clocks, chemicals, and cosmetics.

Many other people work in service industries, or jobs that provide a service for people. Since the end of the 1700s, insurance has been a big business in the state. Hartford remains the home office for seven major insurance firms, such as the Hartford Financial Services Group. Other service industries include financial, telecommunications and information, health care services, real estate, and tourism.

Aetna, one of the largest health insurance companies in America, is a major presence in Hartford.

Coastal Connecticut

Our first stop is Greenwich, in the southwestern corner of Connecticut. At the Audubon Center, you can see a hawk at close range. Thousands of these birds of prey migrate from August through November. The hawks fly along the coast, heading south for the winter.

Stop at Putnam Cottage for a trip to the past. This old inn was built more than 300 years ago. During the Revolutionary War, patriots met there to plot against the British. When British soldiers surprised General Israel Putnam, he escaped from the inn, racing down a cliff on horseback.

Downtown Stamford has shops and outdoor restaurants.

Stamford, located only 38 miles (61 km) from New York City, is Connecticut's fourth largest city. It is named after a community in Lincolnshire, England, the original home of many of New England's early settlers. Today, many of Stamford's 117,083 residents work for big companies such as Xerox and World Wrestling Federation. They ride elevators up to their offices in tall buildings that look like glass towers.

Next, stop in Norwalk to learn about sea creatures in the Long Island Sound. At the Norwalk Maritime Aquarium, you can almost rub noses with sand tiger sharks in a 110,000-gallon (416,395-liter) aquarium. Watch river otters Bell and Sprite splash. Then hop aboard the research boat *Oceanic* to collect marine life. You may catch a squid, a creature with three hearts and a shell on the inside of its body.

The Norwalk Maritime Aquarium offers a close-up look at sharks, as well as seals, otters, and jellyfish.

Bridgeport is Connecticut's largest city, with a population of 139,529. The Beardsley Zoo has 120 kinds of animals roaming in their natural habitat exhibits, including endangered animals such as Siberian tigers. For a hands-on adventure, head to the Discovery Museum. There you can track a comet or reach for the stars in the planetarium. Go on a space mission with the help of a computer. Or wander over to Bridgeport's baseball stadium, the Ball Park at Harbor Yard, and watch the Bluefish play. A member of the Atlantic League of Professional Baseball Clubs, the Bluefish is Bridgeport's own minor league team.

If you've ever been to the circus, you might recognize the name P. T. Barnum. He was once mayor of Bridgeport, where he helped to develop its harbor and parks. However, Barnum is most well-known for starting what is today the Ringling Bros. and Barnum and Bailey Circus or "The Greatest Show on Earth." In the Barnum Museum you can see the carriage that tiny Tom Thumb rode. Although he was only

The Peabody Museum has towering dinosaur skeletons on display.

33 inches (84 cm) tall, Tom Thumb was one of the circus' biggest stars.

Our next stop is New Haven, whose tree-lined streets earned it the nickname "Elm City." President George W. Bush was born in New Haven, where his father (former president George Bush) attended Yale University. More than 10,000 students attend this prestigious school in New Haven. Some of Yale's students have included former president Bill Clinton and actresses Jodi Foster and Claire Danes.

Then get close up to the Apatosaurus skeleton at the Peabody Museum of Natural History. This plant-eating giant weighed about 42 tons. It was 76 feet (23 m) long and 17 feet (5 m) high at its hips. You can also see stuffed birds of every species in the state.

Next take a stroll across the village green—a grassy park. New Haven's green is similar to those in many New England towns. Some greens have bandstands and monuments. Colonists once held meetings, buried their dead, and grazed animals on town greens.

A tour of the coastline wouldn't be complete without going to the beach. At Hammonasset State Park in Madison you can walk on huge boulders that stretch into the ocean. You might also fish for bluefish that travel in schools. If you scuba dive, watch out for jellyfish—they sting when touched. If you're at Hammonasset in May, you can take part in the Sound Winds Kite Festival, when kites soar three stories high.

Continue your tour of the coastline at Old Saybrook. Stop for a sweet snack at James' Soda Fountain, serving up yummy treats since 1896. The drugstore fountain once served up medicines, too. Connecticut's first African-American female pharmacist, Anna James, filled prescriptions there from 1912 to 1967. Next take a cruise on *The African Queen,* a steamboat first used in a movie made in 1951. The movie starred Katharine Hepburn, a famous movie star who lives on Fenwick Island.

Cross over the Thames to Groton and visit the USS *Nautilus* submarine. At the Naval Submarine Base, you can go down the submarine's hatch. Imagine living like sardines as you walk through the control rooms and sleeping area.

Our last stop on this coastal tour is Mystic, once a whaling port. You can spend a day in the nineteenth century at Mystic Seaport. Explore a one-room schoolhouse, or talk with a craftsperson about how to carve a figurehead for the prow of a ship. After playing games of long ago at the

WHO'S WHO IN CONNECTICUT?

Katharine Hepburn (1907–) is a legendary film and stage actress. She starred in many films, including *The African Queen,* and won four Academy Awards—more than any other actress. Hepburn was born in Hartford.

You can take an old-fashioned horse and carriage ride at Mystic Seaport.

children's museum, climb aboard a fleet of tall ships. The last wooden whaling ship in America is anchored here. Built in 1841, the *Charles W. Morgan* and crew chased and harpooned whales.

Save some time to visit with live whales at the Mystic Aquarium. Watch beluga whales and seals play in the outdoor "Alaskan Coast" exhibit. Waterfalls, caves, and rocky beaches make these creatures feel right at home.

East of the Connecticut River

Let's head inland, traveling on the east side of the Connecticut River. We'll take a spin on the Connecticut Turnpike. Look out the window as we pass tiny New England villages and horse farms. Traces of Connecticut's Native Americans can be found in Uncasville. This town honors Chief Uncas, a Mohegan leader and friend of the colonists. Remains of his tribe's fort and burial ground can be seen at Fort Shantok.

Walk through a 1550 native village at nearby Mashantucket, where the Mashantucket Pequot Museum and Research Center lets you explore what life was like for Native American children back then. You can create a musical rain stick or take a cool ride down into a glacial gorge from 18,000 years ago. Go along on a caribou hunt that feels real because of computer animation and sound. Listen to wolves howling as you stand beneath a giant mastodon.

Visitors to the Mashantucket Pequot Museum can wander through a lifelike recreation of an early Pequot village.

North of Mashantucket is Canterbury, where the Prudence Crandall House Museum honors the state's female hero. Crandall started New England's first school for African-American women in 1833. Some townspeople were angry and attacked the school. Crandall was placed on trial twice. All charges were dropped, but the school closed after 18 months because Crandall feared for the safety of her students.

In nearby Storrs, visit the University of Connecticut courtside. The Huskies, a top women's college basketball team, may be practicing hoops and dribbles. At the campus' 1950s soda fountain, you can sample homemade ice cream made from the milk of the university's cows. For almost 50 years, delicious new flavors have been concocted there. Try the Jonathan Supreme, named for UConn's mascot. It is a mixture of vanilla ice cream, chocolate-covered peanuts, and peanut butter swirl.

Heading south, you can find out about live in a mill town by visiting Willimantic. You'll discover what life was like for factory

The UConn Huskies won the NCAA women's basketball national championship in 2002.

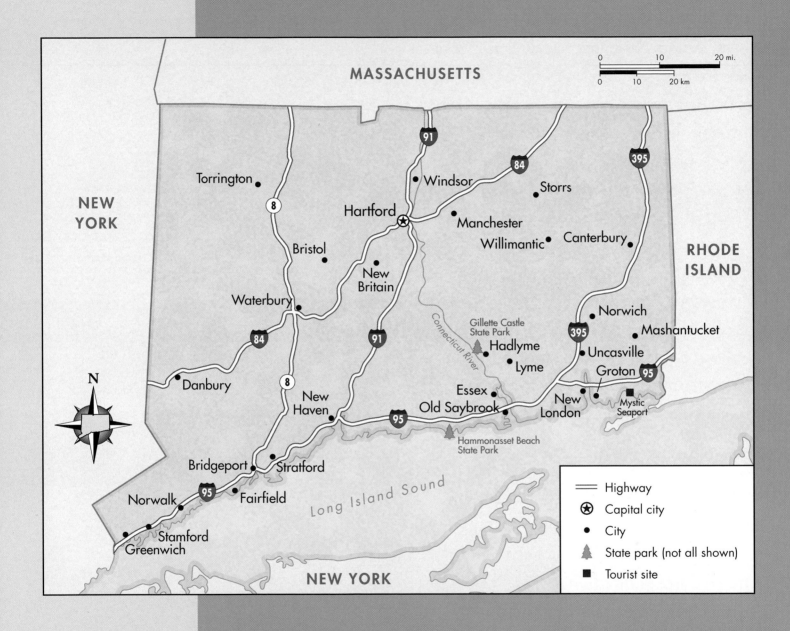

MASSACHUSETTS

NEW YORK

RHODE ISLAND

NEW YORK

Torrington

Windsor

Storrs

Hartford

Manchester

Bristol

Willimantic

Canterbury

New Britain

Waterbury

Norwich

Mashantucket

Gillette Castle State Park

Hadlyme

Danbury

Lyme

Uncasville

Groton

New Haven

Essex

Old Saybrook

New London

Mystic Seaport

Bridgeport

Stratford

Hammonasset Beach State Park

Norwalk

Fairfield

Long Island Sound

Stamford
Greenwich

Connecticut River

N

0   10   20 mi.
0   10   20 km

	Highway
⊛	Capital city
•	City
🌲	State park (not all shown)
■	Tourist site

workers at the Windham Textile and History Museum. Compare the row houses, which were owned by the factory, to the owner's mansion. The thread factory has a fully equipped shop floor and looks just as it did during the height of the Industrial Revolution. In the textile company store, mill workers could buy anything from beef to bonnets, with prices set by the textile company.

Still heading south, let's hop a ferryboat to Hadlyme. Can you spot the castle towering high above the Connecticut River? Actor William Gillette, who played Sherlock Holmes on stage, built his castle from

William Gillette's medieval castle was built in 1919.

Each spring, in colonial New England, Puritans gathered for all-day meetings to elect local officials. This dessert was served during the noon recess, as colonists celebrated casting a vote. Later, in Hartford, colonists munched on this spicy, fruity cake while celebrating an election victory. A recipe appeared in *American Cookery*, the first American cookbook, which was published in Hartford in 1796. The Election Cake recipe in the original cookbook weighed a hefty 90 pounds (41 kg), yielding plenty of leftovers, which the colonists called relics. Don't forget to ask an adult for help!

HARTFORD ELECTION CAKE

1 package dry yeast
1 cup warm water
1/3 cup butter, softened
1/2 cup sugar
1 teaspoon salt
2 eggs
2 teaspoons nutmeg
4-1/2 cups flour
1 tablespoon vanilla
1 cup raisins
confectioners' sugar

1. Preheat the oven to 350°F.
2. Dissolve yeast in water. Add butter, sugar, salt, and eggs. Mix well.
3. Sift nutmeg together with flour. Slowly add dry ingredients to yeast mixture. About halfway through, add vanilla.
4. When mixture becomes too stiff to stir, knead in remaining dry ingredients and raisins. Knead for another 20 strokes.
5. Set the dough to rise in round cake pan until doubled in size (about two hours).
6. Bake the cake for 35 minutes.
7. Cool on wire rack. Sprinkle with confectioners' sugar.

granite. You may get lost in his 24 odd-shaped rooms. No two doors are alike, and each has a special wooden lock. Gillette installed mirrors to watch his friends try to open a secret panel. He hid and had fun spying on them.

East Haddam is home of the Goodspeed Opera House. Built in 1876, the building originally served as a general store, office building, and post office, among other things. Today, this historic building houses a world-class musical theatre.

West of the Connecticut River

Across the river, follow the sound of the steam whistle south to Essex, where you can hop aboard steam locomotives from the 1920s. The Essex Steam Train features original coaches, steam engines, the parlor car, and the Essex Clipper Dinner Train—all rescued from scrap dealers and restored to their original splendor.

New Britain, in central Connecticut, earned the title "Hardware City" because Stanley tools have been made there since the 1850s. Perhaps your family's toolbox has one of Stanley's metal tape measures. Check out some of the original hardware tools manufactured in central Connecticut at the New Britain Industrial Museum. People there also love sports. You can catch a baseball game at the stadium, home of the Rock Cats, or watch the Connecticut Wolves pro-soccer team in action.

If you hear a loud ticking sound, you must be getting close to Bristol. This city once led the nation in clock and watch making. Visit the American Clock and Watch Museum, but don't be alarmed by the

The American Clock and Watch Museum is the first museum in the United States devoted to horology, or the art of making timepieces.

noise when each hour strikes. With more than 1,500 clocks and watches, the museum can get loud. Its clocks date back to the 1590s. If you've always wanted to take one apart, check out clock parts at the old repair shop.

Now let's head south to Waterbury. It is Connecticut's fifth largest city with a population of 107,271. Waterbury was once the brass center of the world. Factories churned out all the brass used for Colorado's Boulder Dam machinery. Step inside the Mattatuck Museum to learn about the city's brass roots, or wander through its nineteenth century brass mill exhibit. In The Connecticut Store, you can buy brass buttons like workers once made. It also sells other items made in the state, such as PEZ® candy and Whiffle® Balls.

Our final stop is a town to the west that became famous for its hats. Factories in Danbury made hats for almost 200 years. The last hat shop closed in 1965, when men's hats fell out of style. You can see hats of all types at the 1790 Dodd Hat Shop, preserved by the Danbury Museum and Historical Society.

Find out how railroads helped shape America at the Danbury Railway Museum. You can hop aboard restored trains, including a steam locomotive, at Union Station. You can also ride in a caboose, learn how to lay track in the rail yard, or find out what different railroad signals mean.

Connecticut is a mixture of cities and small towns, parks, and open land. There's something for everyone in Connecticut.

CONNECTICUT ALMANAC

Statehood date and number: January 9, 1788/5th

State seal: Contains three grapevines to represent the three colonies (New Haven, Saybrook, and Hartford) that merged to form Connecticut. Adopted May 1784.

State flag: Blue silk with a white shield (the state seal) containing three grapevines. Adopted 1897.

Geographic center: Hartford, at East Berlin

Total area/rank: 5,018 square miles (12,997 sq km)/48th

Coastline: 253 miles (407 km)

Borders: Massachusetts, Long Island Sound, Rhode Island, and New York

Latitude and longitude: 40° 58' to 42° 3' N and 71° 47' to 73° 44' W

Highest/lowest elevation: 2,380 feet (725 m) above sea level at Mount Frissell in Salisbury/sea level (Long Island Sound shore)

Hottest/coldest temperature: 106°F (41°C) in Danbury on July 15, 1995/–32°F (–36°C) at Falls Village on February 16, 1943

Land area/rank: 4,845 square miles (12,549 sq km)/48th

Inland water area/rank: 161 square miles (417 sq km)/48th

Population/rank (2000): 3,405,565/29th

Population of major cities:
 Bridgeport: 139,529
 New Haven: 123,626
 Hartford: 121,578
 Stamford: 117,083
 Waterbury: 107,271

Origin of state name: Native Americans called the Connecticut River *Quinnehtukqut*, meaning "beside the long tidal river"

Capital: Hartford

Previous capitals: Hartford and New Haven both served as capital from 1701 to 1875; Hartford became the sole capital in 1875

Counties: 8

State government: 36 senators, 151 representatives

Major rivers/lakes: Connecticut, Farmington, Housatonic, Naugatuck, Quinebaug, Quinnipiac, Shetucket, Thames, Willimantic/Bantam, Lake Candlewood, Twin Lakes

Farm products: Apples, corn, potatoes, tomatoes, tobacco, beef, chicken, eggs, milk, flowers, and shrubs

Livestock: Cattle, poultry

Manufactured products: Aircraft engines, firearms, helicopters, missiles, space hardware, submarines, bearings, brass and copper products, chemicals, clocks, computers, cosmetics, hardware, machine tools, medical instruments, printing machinery, and toys

Mining products: Beryl, crushed stone, feldspar, gravel, mica, red sandstone, sand, and stones

Fishing products: Bass, clams, cod, flounder, lobsters, mackerel, oysters, perch, smelt, swordfish, and trout

Animal: Sperm whale

Bird: American robin

Composer: Charles Edward Ives

Flower: Mountain laurel

Fossil: Eubrontes Giganteus

Hero: Nathan Hale

Heroine: Prudence Crandall

Insect: European mantis

Mineral: Garnet

Motto: *Qui Transtulit Sustinet* (He Who Transplanted Still Sustains)

Nicknames: Constitution State, Provision State, Nutmeg State, Land of Steady Habits

Shellfish: Eastern oyster

Ship: USS *Nautilus*

Song: "Yankee Doodle"

Tree: White oak

Wildlife: Beavers, coyotes, minks, muskrats, opossums, rabbits, raccoons, red foxes, river otters, squirrels, white-tailed deer, woodchuck, bluebirds, crown, great blue herons, hawks, owls, robins, pheasants, quails, ruffed grouse, waterfowl, and woodpeckers

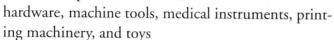

TIMELINE

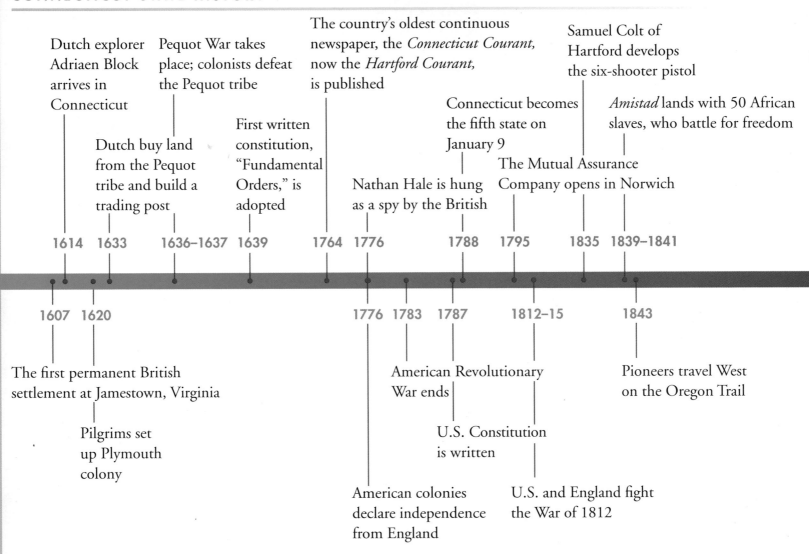

Dutch explorer Adriaen Block arrives in Connecticut

Pequot War takes place; colonists defeat the Pequot tribe

The country's oldest continuous newspaper, the *Connecticut Courant*, now the *Hartford Courant*, is published

Samuel Colt of Hartford develops the six-shooter pistol

Dutch buy land from the Pequot tribe and build a trading post

First written constitution, "Fundamental Orders," is adopted

Connecticut becomes the fifth state on January 9

Amistad lands with 50 African slaves, who battle for freedom

Nathan Hale is hung as a spy by the British

The Mutual Assurance Company opens in Norwich

1614 1633   1636–1637 1639   1764 1776   1788 1795   1835 1839–1841

1607 1620   1776 1783 1787   1812–15   1843

The first permanent British settlement at Jamestown, Virginia

American Revolutionary War ends

Pioneers travel West on the Oregon Trail

Pilgrims set up Plymouth colony

U.S. Constitution is written

American colonies declare independence from England

U.S. and England fight the War of 1812

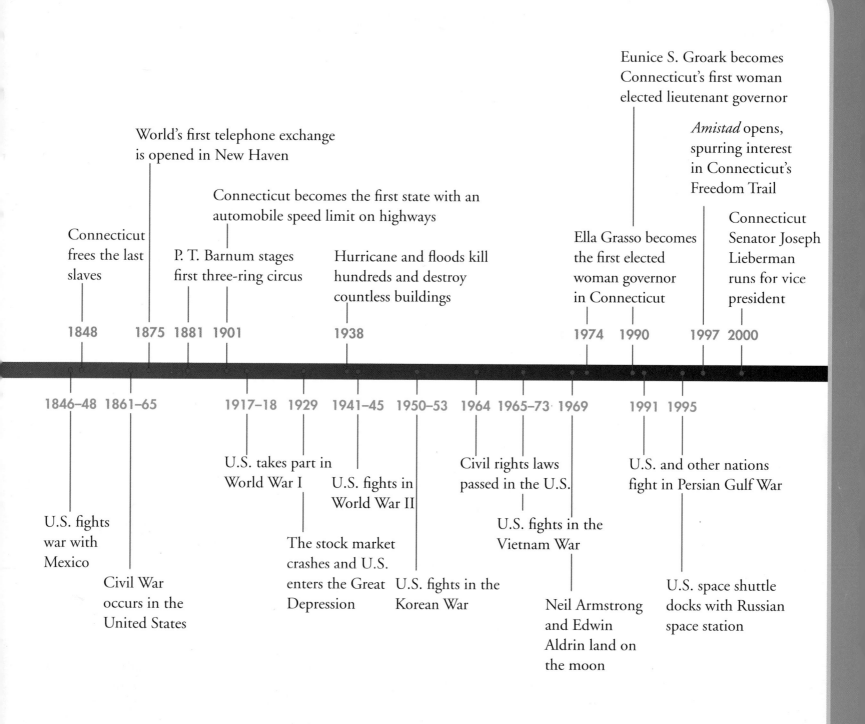

Eunice S. Groark becomes Connecticut's first woman elected lieutenant governor

Amistad opens, spurring interest in Connecticut's Freedom Trail

World's first telephone exchange is opened in New Haven

Connecticut becomes the first state with an automobile speed limit on highways

Connecticut Senator Joseph Lieberman runs for vice president

Connecticut frees the last slaves

P. T. Barnum stages first three-ring circus

Hurricane and floods kill hundreds and destroy countless buildings

Ella Grasso becomes the first elected woman governor in Connecticut

1848   **1875** **1881** **1901**   **1938**   **1974** **1990**   **1997** **2000**

1846–48 **1861–65**   **1917–18** **1929** **1941–45** **1950–53** **1964** **1965–73** **1969**   **1991** **1995**

U.S. takes part in World War I

Civil rights laws passed in the U.S.

U.S. and other nations fight in Persian Gulf War

U.S. fights in World War II

U.S. fights in the Vietnam War

U.S. fights war with Mexico

The stock market crashes and U.S. enters the Great Depression

U.S. fights in the Korean War

Civil War occurs in the United States

Neil Armstrong and Edwin Aldrin land on the moon

U.S. space shuttle docks with Russian space station

GALLERY OF FAMOUS NUTMEGGERS

Marian Anderson
(1897–1993)
Famous opera singer. In 1955, Anderson became the first African-American singer to perform with the Metropolitan Opera. Lived in Danbury.

Phineas Taylor ("P. T.") Barnum
(1810-1891)
Founder of P. T. Barnum's Grand Traveling Circus (called the "Greatest Show on Earth"). It is known today as Ringling Bros. and Barnum and Bailey Circus. He also served as mayor of Bridgeport and in the Connecticut General Assembly. Born in Bethel and lived in Bridgeport.

Caroline B. Cooney
(1947–)
Popular author of young adult books, including the bestselling novel *The Face on the Milk Carton*, which was made into a television movie. Grew up in Old Greenwich and lives in Westbrook.

Dorothy Hamill
(1956–)
Award-winning ice skater. Hamill won a gold medal for women's figure skating in the 1976 Winter Olympics. Born in Riverside.

Calvin Murphy
(1948–)
Known as the Houston Rockets' "Pocket Rocket," he was elected to the Basketball Hall of Fame in 1992. Murphy is regarded as one of the best guards in basketball. Born in Norwalk.

Ralph Nader
(1934–)
A lawyer who ran for president in 2000. A member of the Green Party, Nader has helped get laws passed for health and safety issues, such as safer autos and purer drinking water. Born in Winsted.

Dr. Benjamin Spock
(1903–1998)
A trusted pediatrician (children's doctor) and bestselling author of *The Common Sense Book of Baby and Child Care*, which has sold around the world. Born in New Haven.

Mo Vaughn
(1967–)
Boston Red Sox MVP slugger and 1995 American League Most Valuable Player. In 1999 he signed a 6-year $80 million contract with the Anaheim Angels. Born in Norwalk.

Noah Webster
(1758–1843)
Teacher and lawyer. He became known as "the father of American language" after publishing the first dictionary, *An American Dictionary of the English Language*, in 1828. Born in West Hartford.

GLOSSARY

commemorate: to recall to memory; to remember

compromise: an agreement where both sides give in on several points

constitution: the basic set of laws of a state or nation

delegate: an official representative of a larger group of people

endangered: a plant or animal (or species) whose life is threatened

fundamental: basic; the foundation of something

harness: to control and use (as in a source of power)

hurricane: a giant storm that brings strong winds, rain, thunder, and lightning

independent: free from control by others

industry: a business that produces goods or services

insurance: coverage (usually monetary) against loss of property or life

invention: a new discovery, such as a machine

migrate: to move from one region or climate to another

Nor'easter: a storm with northeast winds, bringing heavy rain or snow

patent: an official document that declares ownership of and the exclusive right to use an invention

patriotism: love for one's country

peninsula: a long finger of land that is surrounded by water on three sides

provisions: supplies

ratify: to confirm or approve

reservoir: a man-made lake in which a large amount of water is stored for use in irrigation or to supply hydroelectric (water) power

FOR MORE INFORMATION

Web sites

Connecticut Historical Society
http://www.chs.org/
Crafts for kids, photo collections.

Connecticut Secretary of the State's Youth World
http://www.sots.state.ct.us/EducationPrograms/
youthworld/YouthWorld.html
Activities for kids and essay contest for fourth grade students.

Exploring *Amistad*
http://amistad.mysticseaport.org/main/welcome.html
Explores the *Amistad* Revolt of 1839–1842.

Historic Ship *Nautilus*
http://www.ussnautilus.org/
Submarine Force Museum, including photos of the *Nautilus.*

Mystic Aquarium/Institute for Explorations
http://www.mysticaquarium.org/
Cool activities for kids and "UnderCurrents" articles.

State of Connecticut
http://www.state.ct.us/scripts/photoall.asp
Photos of the region, animals, and events.

State of Connecticut's ConneCT Kids home page
http://www.kids.state.ct.us/
Information about history, state symbols, and government.

Books

Gelletly, Leeanne. *Harriet Beecher Stowe: Author of Uncle Tom's Cabin* (Famous Figures of the Civil War Era). Broomall, PA: Chelsea House Publishers, 2001.

Lough, Loree. *Nathan Hale: Revolutionary War Leaders.* Broomall, PA: Chelsea House Publishers, 2000.

Newman, Shirlee Petkin. *The Pequots* (Watts Library: Indians of the Americas). Danbury, CT: Franklin Watts, 2000.

Addresses

Connecticut Freedom Trail
Mystic Seaport
Museum of America and the Sea
P. O. Box 6000
Mystic, CT 06355

Connecticut Historical Commission
59 South Prospect Street
Hartford, CT 06106

Connecticut Office of Tourism
505 Hudson Street
Hartford, CT 06106

INDEX

ABOUT THE AUTHOR

Nancy Furstinger grew up listening to childhood memories of summers spent in Connecticut by her mother and her godmother/aunt Marion, who explored their neighborhood on a horse named Nelly. Nancy vacationed at Mystic Seaport, and visited her great aunts Ann and Rose in Connecticut. She discovered wonderful information about their home state through books and the Internet.

A writer since the age of 8, Nancy is also the author of *Catskill Creatures, Creative Crafts for Critters, Fun Stuff with Your Best Friend: The Interactive Dog Book, Let Freedom Ring: The Boston Tea Party*, and *Masters of Music: Irving Berlin*. Nancy and her partner Ken share a mountaintop home in the Catskill Mountains.